First World War
and Army of Occupation
War Diary
France, Belgium and Germany

51 DIVISION
Divisional Troops
Royal Army Veterinary Corps
1/1 Highland Mobile Veterinary Section
1 November 1916 - 1 November 1916

WO95/2860/1

The Naval & Military Press Ltd
www.nmarchive.com
Published in association with The National Archives

Published by

The Naval & Military Press Ltd

Unit 10 Ridgewood Industrial Park,

Uckfield, East Sussex,

TN22 5QE England

Tel: +44 (0) 1825 749494

www.naval-military-press.com

www.nmarchive.com

This diary has been reprinted in facsimile from the original. Any imperfections are inevitably reproduced and the quality may fall short of modern type and cartographic standards.

© Crown Copyright
Images reproduced by permission of The National Archives, London, England, 2015.

Contents

Document type	Place/Title	Date From	Date To
Heading	51st (Highland) Division 51st Mobile Vety Section May 1915-1919 Mar		
Heading	War Diary For The Month Of February 1916 Of The 1/1st Highland Mobile Vet Section 51st Division Vol II		
Heading	War Diary Of 1/1st High Mobile Vet Sect. 51st Division For March 1916 Vol III		
Heading	War Diary For Month Of April 1916 of 1st High Mobile Veterinary Section 51st Division.		
Heading	War Diary Of 1/1st High M.V.S 51st Div For The Month Of May 1916.		
Heading	War Diary Of 1/1st High M.V.S 51st Div For Month Of June 1916 A.C Burton Capt A.V.C O.C 1/1 High M.V.S. 51st Div.		
Heading	War Diary Of 1/1st High M.V.S. 51st Division for Month of July 1916 A.C Burton Capt A.V.C O.C. 1/1st High M.V.S. 51st Div.		
Heading	War Diary Of 1/1st High MVS 51st Division For Month Of August 1916 Vol 8		
Heading	War Diary Of 1/1st (Highland) Mobile Veterinary Section 51st Division For Month Of September 1916 Vol 9		
Miscellaneous	To D.A.G. G.H. Quarters 3rd Echelon	01/11/1916	01/11/1916
Heading	War Diary For The Month Of November 1916 1/1 Highland Mobile Veterinary Section 51st Division A.C. Burton Capt. A.V.C.		
Heading	War Diary For The Month Of December 1916 1/1 Highland Mobile Veterinary Section 51st Division A.C. Burton Capt. A.V.C. Vol 12		

51ST (HIGHLAND) DIVISION

51ST MOBILE VETY SECTION
MAY 1915 - FEB 1919
1919 MAR

51ST (HIGHLAND) DIVISION

War Diary for the Month of
February 1916.
Of the
1/1st Highland Mobile Vet. Section
51st Division.
Vol II

War Diary of 1/1st High Mobile Vet. Sect.

51st Division

for

March 1916

Vol III

War Diary for Month of April 1916
of
1/1st High. Mobile Veterinary Section
51st Division.

A. C. Burton Capt. A.V.C
O.C 1/1st High M.V.S.
51st Div.

War Diary of 1/1st High M.V.S.
51st Div
for the month of May 1916.

ORIGINAL

War Diary of 1/1st High. M.V.S
51st Div.
for
Month of June 1916.

A.C. Burton Capt. A.V.C.
O.C. 1/1 High. M.V.S.
51st Div.

ORIGINAL

War Diary of 1/1st High M.V.S.
51st Division
for Month of July 1916

A.C. Burton   Capt. R.V.C.
                  O.C. 1/1st High M.V.S.
                  51st Div.

ORIGINAL

Vol 8

War Diary of 1/1st High MVS
51st Division
for
Month of August 1916

A.C. Burton, Capt A.V.C.
O C 1/1st High MVS
51st Div.

51

Not With See Original.
Vol 9

War Diary of 1/1st (Highland)
Mobile Veterinary Section.
51st Division.
for Month of September 1916.

A.C Burton   Capt R.V.C.
             O.C 1/1st High.M.V.S.
             51st Division

1/1st HIGHLAND MOBILE VET. SECT.
No.
Date 5.10.16
61st DIVISION

To. D.A.Q.
G.H. Quarters,
3rd Echelon.

Herewith War Diary for month of October, 1916, please.

A.C. Burton — Capt. A.V.C.
O.C. 1/1st (H) Mobile Vety Sect,
51st Division.

Vol 10 51

To
D.A.G.
G.H.Quarters,
3rd Echelon

War Diary for month of
October, 1916.

A C Burton Capt. A.V.C.
OC 1/1st (High) Mobile
Veterinary Section
51st Division

CONFIDENTIAL.
No 21/A.
HIGHLAND DIVISION.

Original Copy

War Diary

for the month of November 1916

1/1 Highland Mobile Veterinary Section

51st Division

A.C. Burton Capt. A.V.C.

Vol 12

CONFIDENTIAL.
No. 21(A)
HIGHLAND DIVISION.

Original Copy

War Diary

for the month of

December 1916.

1/1 Highland Mobile Veterinary Section

51st Division

A.C. Burton Capt. A.V.C.

www.ingramcontent.com/pod-product-compliance
Lightning Source LLC
Chambersburg PA
CBHW081513160426
43193CB00014B/2676